THIS IS ME

I'm Adopted

Fiona Myles

This Is Me
I'm Adopted

Authored by Fiona Myles
© Fiona Myles 2022
Cover Design: Marcia M Publishing House
Cover Photography: Fiona Myles
Edited by Marcia M Publishing House Editorial Team, Lee Dickinson
Published by Marcia M Spence of Marcia M Publishing House,
West Bromwich, West Midlands the UNITED KINGDOM B71 on behalf of
Fiona Myles
All rights reserved 2022 Marcia M Publishing House

The author has recreated events, locales and conversations from her memories of them. In order to maintain anonymity in most instances the author has changed the names of individuals and places and may have changed some identifying characteristics and details such as physical properties, occupations and places of residence.

www.marciampublishing.com

ACKNOWLEDGMENTS

I want to acknowledge first and foremost that without God being in my life you would not be reading this book.

I want to give honour to my parents Patsy and Bobby Cochrane who had an awful time with me but never gave up on me. I sometimes wonder if they had known about Adoption Trauma would things have been different? Who knows?

To my brother Gavin - You are the best brother

To my sister Mhairi - You are the best sister

Thank you to both of you for all that you had to put up with when I was in the madness and thank you both for supporting me through getting my story out to the world. I love you both very much.

To my church Victory Outreach Manchester - I can't single out anyone as the acknowledgements would be longer than the book.

To all those at The Peoples Church Falkirk again I can't single anyone out but thank you for nurturing me as a baby Christian. And then letting me go into Victory Outreach after 6 years.

FOREWORD

Since writing this book I received my adoption files which blew my whole thinking to bits. Nothing was as it had been told to me by my birth family. I have dealt with it and have been processing the findings.

This book and my first book This is Me - No Darkness Too Deep has been a labour of love.

I had an incident at work that caused me to realise that I had so many unresolved issues even after many, many years as a Christian.

Covid and lockdown brought me to a place where I knew I had to write my story. Both books were written within the year with a solid nudge from Tarnya Coley. Thank you Tarnya. Over the course of getting book one out into the world, I had professional counselling which was incredible.

As an adoptee, I've come to realise after all this time that there IS such a thing as Adoption Trauma. During the past few months, I have been connecting with adoptees and adopters from all over the world and finding out that this is nothing new and so many adoptees have the same struggles.

We struggle with things that are not unique to adoptees but are heightened by being adopted. This book was the most difficult to write as I had to revisit catalytic moments in my life where my head exploded because I was adopted. Then I went on a journey of self-destruction, as documented in book one.

Both books bring hope, both books bring honesty and a candid look at life as a non-Christian and life as a Christian. I have been a Christian for over 25 years. Some of those years in Pastoral Leadership and many not. Through my first book, I have seen people come to know Christ and some come back to Him. The heart behind the books is one of compassion and reaching out to adoptees. Especially older adoptees who may not have had the support as youngsters in dealing with the emotional turmoil that being adopted can bring. I'm not saying that all adoptees are the same, some that I have met seem to have no issues at all. But as for me and my story...

I have also documented my 33 years of infertility and my miraculous gift of a child when I was 50. I do hope this book is helpful to you the reader.

You're Chosen, Special, You're Adopted

"**M**ummy, why do you have little holes in your ears?" I was sitting in the sink in our kitchen getting my evening washdown. My mother had patiently and painstakingly explained that I was adopted, chosen, and special, wanted more than anything. To say that I hadn't been listening was a bit of an understatement. I wasn't getting what she was trying to tell me as my focus was on the holes in her ears.

My parents had been advised in the 1960s, when I was adopted, to tell me as early as possible, even as a baby, that I was chosen, special and adopted. This occasion is the first one I can remember, when I was six. Those three words were constantly applied to my life and I really don't like being called special; the word still gets on my nerves to this day when applied to me.

Fifty-five years later (and it could be longer by the time you read this), I wish they had been told to wait until I was an adult and able to deal with all the emotion that it brought with it. I do often question whether things would have been better, the same or worse than they were had I been told at a more adult age. Would my life have spiralled out of control the way it did if I had not been given these three words to cart around with me for the rest of my childhood, never really knowing what to do with the burden of being special, chosen and adopted? I did not have the tools to deal with all that being adopted brought with it.

There were so many huge questions for a small child. *Where are my mummy and daddy that didn't want me? Why did they not want me? What did I do to be thrown aside as an unwanted child?*

The weight of being adopted was for me like carrying around a huge bag of stones all the time. The older I got, the heavier the burden became. I struggled inside with my identity, struggled with really frightening, huge waves of pain and fear. Then, to put a tin lid on the whole sorry mess, my hormones decided to kick in early. My mind exploded with emotion and hormone imbalance enough to kick a grown man into orbit, never mind a scared little girl who, by that time, was becoming the cuckoo in the nest. I didn't feel connected to my family; I felt awkward, different, strange, and I was.

Throughout my childhood I always felt different and, to be fair, I was a bit different. I was the little specky kid that wasn't afraid to say the things other people thought. I made pals with people quickly, always trying to impress and find some sort of connection.

My mother was a teacher and became a headteacher at a school for children with special needs. My father was a prison officer and became the governor of a prison. They were great parents. I had an older brother who was four years older than me. He was too cool. I idolised him. I had a younger sister who was pretty and smiley with cute, curly hair. I was smack-bang in the middle of their two biological children, which is probably worst-case scenario stuff; a middle child tends to have issues anyway, never mind being the adopted, chosen, special child in the middle. It was a recipe for the destruction that was to come.

We lived in a small village in Scotland. An idyllic setting of hills, woods, fields and rivers were our playground. The village had a park and some extremely tempting ruined coal mines that we were always told not to go near as they were dangerous and there were the ghosts and skeletons of the men that had died in the mines when they blew up. As to how true any of the stories of skeletons and ghosts were, I don't know, but it made for great adventures in the mines trying to scare each other half to death.

As a young child, I was always getting into trouble doing something bizarre. I took a teddy that was my sister's favourite and went round the village taking 5p off people to guess its name. When I was caught out, which wasn't hard as the village was so small, word got around really quickly as to what I had been up to with said teddy. My brother had to walk around with me to everyone's house to give all the money back and to get the teddy back.

Was I just showing a bit of entrepreneurship or was I being bad? I was always getting into trouble for one thing or another, so the words "bad" and "evil" were bandied about quite regularly. I didn't realise I was I was just being the way I was as a fairly disturbed young girl not coping with the news that I was adopted, special and chosen. I sat through many lectures on the perils of not turning over a new leaf. My mum and dad were at pains to continually tell me I was special, chosen, and being adopted was something really good. It just wasn't good in my world, on the inside.

We had a fantastic time as kids: holidays, weekends away in the caravan, birthdays were amazing, Christmas was always huge with all the trimmings. Aunties, uncles, grannies and granddads were all lovely. My nana and grandad had a poodle called Puffles. This dog will live in my memory even when I'm dead. It was the grumpiest little dog ever. I think if it was able to speak it would have asked my nana not to let us children into the house to wind it up. I liked grumpy Puffles.

My nana was a formidable woman; she was nobody's fool and ran her house with a rod of steel. For me, she was firm but fair and I loved going to her house to stay, especially on my own. I liked being wanted and needed. Nana used to let me run up and down the stairs taking care of my granddad, taking his food up and the dirty plate back down, helping him get his tablets out. She used to go to the bingo at night and leave me in with Granddad. He would bang on the floor and I would run up to see what he needed. He would ask where Nana was and I would tell him she was sleeping in the chair or over at Mrs Harvey's across the road. I would make the toast and lime marmalade and make the tea he was asking for, feeling very grown-up and needed. Times at Nana's were great.

By the time I had reached thirteen years of age, things were getting very much worse. I had been steadily getting into trouble doing outrageous things: stealing from the neighbours, being cheeky and out of order at school. I had stolen my brother's paper money, raided Mum's purse, among other things. There are too many misdemeanours to go through, and I had started some bizarre behaviours.

Being adopted for me was not a good experience on the inside, but a solid, good, stable upbringing was the upside of it. My parents were great. I put them through really trying times and, at one point, Mum was on Valium to help her cope with my behaviour.

Things came to a head after I tried to kill my little sister for the second time, which is detailed in my first book *This is Me: No Darkness Too Deep*, and had been caught with a knife roaming around the house at night. I was referred to a psychiatrist. I can vaguely remember going to see him and the dark, dark room he was in. Mum went with me and came in at first, then waited outside while I was supposed to be answering his questions. I just wouldn't speak to him. He prescribed diazepam for me, to be crushed into my food in the evening to ensure I slept through the night. My night-time wanderings were becoming a real problem. I had started to hurt myself as well.

I joked with Mum later on in life that it was her fault I ended up on drugs for giving me a taste of it when I was young.

So what was wrong with me? I had tons of issues: abandonment, I was fearful, insecure, had rejection issues. You name it, I seemed to have it all rolled up on the inside of me while, on the outside, trying to maintain a semblance of normality and respectability to not bring shame to my parents. Even with my best efforts, I wasn't able to maintain any sort of good behaviour.

There were the odd teachers at high school that did make attempts to connect with me. I was good at athletics, running and non-contact sports. I had a good head for numbers and did well in English classes. Each year in high school the teachers changed, which was a problem for me. It took me almost the whole year to get to grips with the teacher or, in some cases, not get to grips with the teacher. Then, moving from the first year into the second year, almost all the teachers changed, which was a nightmare for me.

I lost my temper and often had a real lack of self-control when the buttons were pushed. It was never my fault; all I could see was people being hard on me and not taking the time to help me or attempt to help me.

I knew I was in trouble, big trouble on the inside, but was unable to articulate it to anyone. So out it came in angry, explosive, sneaky, ugly behaviour. I was lying, stealing and fighting with anyone who annoyed me. Always pushing people away, but always wanting, desiring to be in some kind of group of girls apart from the bad girls. I so dearly wanted to be like the nice girls with nice hair and tidy uniforms that everyone liked. In saying that, it was not my group either.

I desperately wanted to connect. I wanted to feel I belonged even to the class I was in. I fluttered around all the groups of girls trying to find an 'in', but most didn't want me around. I gravitated towards loners who were either strange or lost or new.

I did make one very solid connection with a girl called Anne who had a great family. She was a late baby, the only girl in a family of boys. Her mum was the cutest, sweetest little lady who I thought was just the perfect mum. We stayed friends throughout school and remain friends to this day. She was wild and so was I. We got up to some real mischief. Anne was so funny and grown-up. She taught me to squeeze myself into skintight, shiny trousers with the help of a strong metal coat hanger! She also showed me how to play a record backwards to hear other messages in it. Probably because she had lots of big brothers, she just seemed to be so grown-up. She smoked cigarettes, so I decided to smoke too. I thought I was going to die outright on my first two or three attempts at smoking. It was truly horrible, but I wanted to fit in with what Anne did.

We were boy daft. Two epic memories of the silly things we did were joining a karate club in Clackmannan because Anne fancied someone. All I got out of that whole few weeks of doing karate were a few bruises and sore muscles and the ability to block a punch. We had boyfriends in Menstrie: two likely lads that thought they were on to a good thing. Anne was staying over at mine for the weekend, my mum and dad had gone to the club and my brother was supposed to be babysitting us. We managed to get all dolled up and sneaked out the back to walk down to meet our 'boyfriends'. On the way down the hill we were singing 'Billy Don't Be a Hero' at the top of our lungs when my dad pulled up in the car; he was heading the same way to pick up another couple that were going to the club. I nearly died of fright right on the spot. He was furious, jumped out of the car and barked at us to get in the car. My heart was beating out of my chest. I knew I was going to get it. We got home and, with lots of threats, Dad went upstairs and came back down with different trousers on. Mum told me years later that he had been so shocked at catching us all dolled up heading out that he had dropped his lit cigarette on the seat of the car. He had sat on said lit cigarette when he got back in the car, burning his bum and a hole in his trousers. That still makes me laugh, even now, writing it.

My mental state was not good and school became a horrible place for me. I always felt that no one liked me and that everyone was laughing at me. I did stupid things to get negative attention, not realising I just needed someone to talk to. My parents were at their wits' end with me and I was getting into more and more trouble. Certain phrases like 'we are ashamed of you', 'we chose you', 'you're special', etc. began to seep in, saying to me that I needed to be repaying them for their kindness, not being a nutjob and spoiling their family. In my traumatised state I was hearing one thing and they thought they were saying another.

I began to want to get out of the house. I needed them to send me back to my real mum. Surely she would understand me, would know what was wrong with me? My birth mum was Maggie, who had given birth to me in March 1966. By June 1966, I had gone to live with my auntie and, by October 1966, I was in an orphanage waiting to be chosen.

I knew without a shadow of a doubt I wasn't normal. I knew I wasn't evil, as was often said. But then the realisation would seep in that, of course, my real mum wouldn't know what was wrong with me; she didn't even care enough about me as a baby to try to keep me. I knew from an early age that I had an older sister and that absolutely did my head in. Every time I thought about it, which was almost all the time, I got so angry that I had been chucked into an orphanage and she had been kept. What on earth do you think that said to me all my little life? I was not good enough to be kept and, oh, look, the proof was in the pudding. Who would want this twisted, weird, bad child anyway? Had she kept me, she would most likely have given me away anyway because of the way I had turned out.

I always wondered what my sister looked like. Did she look like me? Was she a lunatic as well? Did she have problems? Did she know about me and wonder what I was like? My head was like a bubbling cauldron all the time, and then it would bubble over, spilling out into hot arguments, heated fights, words that would burn. I had so many fights around the village and at school; some I won and some I didn't. I got so angry so quickly and lashed out without a thought. I would find myself in the staff room covered in someone else's blood regretting it already. I went up fast but always simmered down very quickly as well.

There was a feeling always that no one liked me or wanted to be my friend. I went to other people's houses and soon wasn't invited back for some reason or another. The thing was I went around all the time with my buddy: trouble.

My brother joined the RAF and went away to do his training. I missed him a lot; he was my hero. He had a girlfriend called Sheena that lived around the corner from us. She was OK. I knew her from the housing estate we lived in and from school. He was due to come home one weekend but had been delayed. I had gone round to let her know, and she was out on the street with some of her friends as I bumbled up and told her he wasn't coming home as planned. She laughed and said out loud to her friends, "What on earth would she know? She's only adopted, not his real sister."

That moment of utter devastation has to be one of the most profoundly damaging sentences I heard as a child. To think that's how people who didn't even really know me were talking about me. I wasn't even really considered to be a part of the family that had adopted me. What a truly cruel and heartless and completely ignorant thing to say to a child in the street in front of people. I can't remember the ins and outs of what happened next, but I know I went for her. My brother dumped her for saying it, endorsing his hero status in my heart. But I had to put up with her nasty comments for months after that drama. It stayed with me that people outside my family didn't see me as being a valid member of the family.

My inner being was a crippled little girl growing into a woman's body. I didn't fit emotionally or intellectually into my shape and size. There I was a little girl stuck, unable to grasp adulthood correctly, to connect correctly with people. Always afraid of being cut off, rejected, left out unwanted. Let the battle commence.

I went at seventeen, out into the big bad world, a messed-up individual with a great moralistic and secure upbringing, all the correct things taught to me, rights and wrongs, good manners and everything. But on the inside I was a seething mass of anger, pain, fear and rejection.

Don't misunderstand where I'm coming from. I had some excellent times with my family. Holidays were always epic. We had fun nights in the village if there was a power cut doing a little turn on the soapbox. A little song or imitating someone off *Coronation Street*.

We were very well looked after. We were all given chores to do, taught how to cook, iron our clothes, etc. Our mum was a mummy mum and our dad was a daddy dad. I truly loved them both dearly, and my brother and sister. We had laughs, we had rows, like all fairly normal families.

One of my favourite things was coming home from school and seeing the caravan on the drive, which meant we were going somewhere for the weekend. It was a fairly military operation getting the caravan filled and ready to go.

Still, in all of it, I struggled. Sometimes Mum would talk to me about being adopted, obviously intending to help but usually just making more questions I couldn't answer and neither could she. I was told occasionally I was having a much better life than if I had stayed with my natural family. That kind of statement only led me to think they knew something about my family and how they were. All terribly confusing. I daydreamed about this amazing family, where they all smiled sweetly at me and wanted to get to know me. The moment of meeting them, what would that be like? What if they didn't want to know me? What if they died and I never knew they had died? I wasn't even really sure I wanted to meet someone who didn't actually want me. I didn't know if I wanted to meet the sister who had been saved from adoption, rejection and abandonment because she was obviously loved so much more than me. Surely that was a no-brainer, that there must have been something wrong with me when I was born?

Debilitating stuff to think about, never mind try to process. And what if there were more brothers and sisters – how would I get on with them? Did any of them know about me? What if I was just some sordid secret and that was why I had been given away? Maybe a married man's child? Oh the shame of it in the 60s, and in a tiny village to boot. She would have been the talk of the steamie, as the Scots would say.

I can understand as an adult why I was given up. It doesn't make it feel any better, but I do know the backstory now.

Adoption

I can see the need for adoption. I understand there are some people who, for whatever reason, need to put their children up for adoption. I also know, being someone who was unable to have children for thirty-three years, adoption may well have been the only option for me to have a child. It wasn't an option for me though, as I always said to myself I would never adopt a child, as I wouldn't want to be the cause of a child going through what I went through, not being able to deal with being adopted. My hubby always said he didn't want to adopt either, so at least we were on the same page on that one. The thought of having to watch a child navigate the swamp of feelings they have once they know they are adopted was not something I ever wanted to face.

It's fair to say not all adoptions are good, but not all are bad. It is also fair to say all adoptees have to navigate their feelings on being adopted. Some manage fairly well and some barely manage to get through life, and anywhere else within those two parameters is on the scale.

In my case, I had the added burden of being sandwiched between two natural kids. Both are super-clever and super-nice. Neither wore glasses, whereas I did, adding to the awkwardness of being me. Would being adopted now have made a difference to how I was as a child? I don't know, to be honest. It's possible, as there are lots of support groups and a recognition of certain traits that we, as adoptees, have. I maybe would have been able to get a mentor or a buddy that could have stuck by me to help me through the stormy emotions.

I used to think it would have been better if I had never been told I was adopted, believing I was just their kid. But then what does finding out as an adult do to you? I imagine I would have twigged I was a bit different anyway.

It's such a minefield of emotions on all sides. I sometimes think about how my mum and dad must have felt choosing me. Did they at any point think to themselves, 'I wish I had chosen the kid on the second bed from the left that was sleeping peacefully instead of the crazy kid with the crazy hair that was bouncing up and down with the big smile'? It's not a question I have the answer to. I think, if I'm honest, it's probably something I would have thought if it was me as the adopter. Sorry if that offended anyone.

Becoming a Christian

Becoming a Christian in 1996 most certainly helped me get through some of the trauma of the awful things that happened to me in my late teens and early twenties. I was able to receive prayer and pray through the pain and confusion that had built up in my mind; my heart began to heal from a lot of the pain of adoption. It's such a struggle to be in the middle all the time with the feelings that I have. I struggle to be open about how I am really feeling and allow things to build up inside of me because I don't want to express how sensitive I am to certain things being said.

In my early years as a Christian, I took so long to get up and running with my prayer life and understanding grace and mercy that I know I side-swerved really looking at all the adoption issues. I felt God had done such great work on all the other issues that I was grateful to not be using drugs or alcohol to cover how I was truly feeling. Yet that struggle was still there to a certain degree. My life was trotting along at a fairly good pace doing the things I truly enjoyed, which were working with women, and prayer. My prayer life was great. I enjoyed praying with the team and I enjoyed praying on my own. Leading other people in prayer was great.

Often I would get into that place where I would be prompted to look at why I was feeling jealous or hurt by a situation that didn't seem to be that big an issue, but something else would come up and be of more immediate importance, so for years the adoption stuff never got looked at and, eventually, it seemed to get buried under a whole lot of life.

So what are the top ten things that adopted people struggle with?

1) Rejection

2) Fear

3) Abandonment issues

4) Relationships

5) Connections

6) Pain

7) Jealousy

8) Hypersensitivity

9) Unusual triggers

10) Staying in one place

This list can be much more extensive but, in the research I have done, these came out as the top ten issues adoptees seem to really struggle with. We can act out our pain and fears in such bizarre ways and not understand why other people don't get where we are coming from. As a kind of disclaimer, I have come across many adoptees who are fairly well adjusted to their adoption processing. This did cause me to also look at someone's personality as a factor in why they might not be able to process their adoption well. Is it the age they were adopted at that makes a difference as to how they are going to process? Or is it the family they are brought up in that makes their processing different? I'm still looking into that.

Finding Nemo – No, Not Really

Getting back to us adoptees that have struggled for years on the processing part of our adoptions, I want to ask the question: what is it that you think would make you better? Are you always yearning for something to make you better, to find that missing link that will put everything right?

I thought that finding my natural family would have slotted all that was wrong back into place. I was wrong. It certainly helped me to see that some of my issues were actually hereditary and some were from being adopted. So it is worth looking at whether some of the things you are struggling with are to do with your biological parentage.

It was a moment I will never forget, making that first phone call to my natural granny. The poor lady was utterly distressed and happy all at once. I hadn't been a sordid secret or anything, which helped in the meeting-up stages. The family had been waiting from the moment I turned eighteen, searching for the papers to see if I was looking for them and things like that.

My parents drove me to the town where I was to meet my natural mum and I had packed an overnight bag to stay the weekend if the initial meeting went well. My mum and dad were going to come back and pick me up on Monday but had said they would stay and go round the shops for a couple of hours in case I didn't like the situation and wanted to go home straight away. There were no mobile phones in those days. I just knew they would be there until 4 p.m.

Going Back to the Top Ten Struggles Adoptees Can Face:

Rejection – Sometimes I feel my whole life has been one big rejection.
– Marilyn Monroe

Do not waste yourself in rejection; do not bark against the bad, but chant the beauty of the good.
– <u>Ralph Waldo Emerson</u>

The meaning of the word rejected is 'not given approval or acceptance'.

We experience feelings of rejection in our lives even if we are not adopted. My husband suffers dreadfully with real feelings of rejection. It doesn't cripple him inside the way it does me. It takes me a while to bounce back from rejection and being rejected. After twelve weeks of being here on the planet, I was taken to my aunt's to be looked after. Nine weeks later I was in an orphanage. I was adopted from there within another eight weeks. In my mind, how on earth would a baby remember any of this or have such strong feelings of rejection and fear from it?

After speaking to many experts on this subject, I now know that, as babies, smell is vital to us recognising where we are and who we are with. So, for me, my baby brain had to deal with that change three times. I was fascinated to find out just how much smell is a huge factor in a baby's security.

Fear – this has played a huge part in my life all my life. I can be afraid of what may happen, making up fantasies in my mind, creating situations where there wasn't a situation, deciding that someone is out to get me when they barely even know me. I can be hyper-aware of anything that may be a danger to me. This was always there in my childhood as a running theme and I would lash out in the moment of panic, thinking something bad was going to happen to me. I struggled to relax, always looking around to see what dangers lay around the corner. My fears and concerns, I have found, are all directly related to being adopted. Straight away fear is deep inside us, as we are very aware that things can change very quickly and, as children, we do not have the ability to express the feelings overwhelming us.

Definition of fear – an unpleasant, often strong emotion caused by anticipation or awareness of danger

Adoption – legally made the son or daughter of someone other than a biological parent

Adoption is a legal and binding contract. You are becoming parents to someone else's child. What if the biological parents' circumstances changed and they were going to be able to manage to keep you? You are never going to find out; you are legally bound to the adopters. From my own story, I was not aware of the legalities, but was always told I could not even begin to look for my natural family until I was at least eighteen, and even then would need to speak to a professional. The systems when I was young did not work very well. I do not recall even knowing what a social worker was, never mind actually meeting one. We just bobbed along.

Connections – the state of being connected

Connected – joined or linked together

Connections, for me, have been so difficult to maintain. I can stay in touch with people and maintain contact. I can also keep other people in contact with each other. I think about other people and text, email or call to stay in contact – there is a huge difference between staying in contact with someone and being connected to someone. As an adoptee, I have always been able to stay completely disconnected from things and from most people. I have always been able to leave everything behind and move on with just one or two favoured pieces of clothing. I used to flit from place to place like a little bird landing in a tree and sitting for a little while, but then that little birdie would need to quickly move to another tree as some imminent danger was about to attack. Always flitting from place to place, trying desperately to find my nesting place, and so the trail of fear and uncertainty goes on and on, year after year, not really being able to understand why I can't stop and stay or nest anywhere I go. I meet people I would like to connect with but I am inherently unable to make that link, that bonding that will scratch that itch. Connecting is unbelievably difficult for me.

My book *This is Me: No Darkness Too Deep* details my awful journey from disaster to disaster looking for connection, looking for love, wondering what love is. *What does it feel like? How will I know I've found it?*

I thought I had found it in my first husband; he saved me from certain death. We had lots of laughs but also had lots of bad times. Eventually, he went off with another woman, something he had already done. He wasn't faithful in marriage, but did I want to make a fuss? No, not really. I thought marriage was for life and was so shocked to be on my own and divorced.

Off I went at high speed into another tailspin of destruction, settling into a flat in Glasgow and finding husband number two. He was a more settled character, but it's still a crazy set of memories of visiting prisons, passing drugs, drinking and being violent (that was me, not him). I liked being with him. I came to the point in my life where I became a Christian and he didn't. This ended with him getting a woman pregnant and leaving me to live happily ever after and, again, I was left on my own. Major connections smashed in my life yet again. These marital disasters were again causing rejection, fear and loss and again not wanting to connect fully with anyone.

Infertility played a huge part in my adult life. The first time I was pregnant was at seventeen. I didn't even know I was pregnant. I had been badly beaten by a partner and woke up in hospital to the news that I had lost my child, a boy, at twenty weeks. I named him Thomas in my head. Another loss. I wondered and wondered for years what my life would have looked like if I had that child. Would it have changed everything? Would it have given me that longed-for connection I was failing to make anywhere else?

- **Connection quote – "We are hard-wired to connect with others. It is what brings purpose and meaning to our lives and without it there is suffering." – Brené Brown**
- **Jealousy quote – "You can only be jealous of someone who has something you think you ought to have yourself." – Margaret Atwood**

OK, hands up: who admits to being jealous? It's not one of those things we hear many saying, that they are steeped in deep-rooted jealousy. As an adoptee, I can say that jealousy was a huge dark place in my heart even as a small child. I was jealous of people who had nice family connections – basically anyone who wasn't adopted. It's so hard for me to put into words, and I'm trying so hard.

I had a wonderful childhood with lots of happy times. I wasn't subjected to anything untoward. We didn't see our parents drinking except at the new year or at a wedding. We never faced any repercussions from our parents drinking. We didn't grow up in poverty, had everything we needed and more; we had a nanny, cleaner and someone came and did our hair. We always had warm winter coats and boots and lovely holidays in the summer.

So, why all the jealousy? Because I wanted more than anything else not to be adopted. I wanted to be like everyone else. I don't remember knowing anyone else who was adopted. It was like a really bad word for me. Growing up in a very small village wasn't helpful. By way of explanation, there were only a few families living there, and none of them I knew of had anyone adopted. It was idyllic in the sense of location, though, and it's the one place I truly loved living in.

Loneliness is one of the most prevalent feelings in my life; being stuck between wanting to reach out but not feeling able to. I fight through this daily. It's vital to me to make myself connect with someone at some point in every day or I would happily choose not to connect at all.

Feelings of never being good enough are something that I struggle hugely with as an adoptee. I believe this stems from feeling different and being different.

The Little Girl in a Woman's Body: Lost in Adulthood

Exploring some of the areas where we fall short is often something that we choose not to do. What if we did come out as who we really are? What if we allowed ourselves to overcome all the feelings we have? Our feelings are not right and neither are they wrong, but the key is they are just feelings and we so very often allow them to lead us into unknown paths where we were never destined to travel. I have acted on my feelings in more negative situations than positive ones over the years and recently, in my newfound freedom from being bound up in self-pity, self-destruction and self-preservation, I can see how darkly lit my path has been over the last few years. It's almost as if there were blinkers over my eyes. All I could see and feel was the pain of loss after loss adding to the layers of unresolved pain already there. I never understood until not long ago why I struggle so much with loss – why could I not process loss properly? In particular the loss of people through death. I am not attached to things, pictures, knick-knacks, etc. I can easily leave things behind without a second thought. That unattached feeling is something I thought was just the way I was; I didn't connect it to being adopted. Almost all the feelings I've struggled with over the years are connected to being adopted but, for me, for many years I thought a lot of them were down to my nomadic lifestyle, which in itself was down to being adopted.

So many paths I have stumbled down over the years thinking, 'This time all will be well. I've found what I'm looking for, be that a partner, a place or a home or a friend.' In every circumstance, I've been standing in utter disbelief that this venture has not worked and this person doesn't actually like me, never mind love me. In workplaces, I've always not been in anyone's camp, but in everyone's camp, in case I get kicked out of the camp!

Over the years I've been told I need counselling. I went for counselling on a few occasions but was never able to fully relax and/or share honestly about where I was at or how I was feeling.

As a Christian, I have always been more than able to believe for others in terrible situations. I've seen God move in many people's lives as I've prayed earnestly for their healing and spiritual growth, but always on my knees knowing that there is something missing from my own life/heart/spirit.

Many times I have spoken to other Christians trying to explain the way I feel, but most times are just given trite comments of, "Oh I know how you're feeling; I've felt like that when XYZ happened." Inside I'm screaming, *you are not hearing me. You may think you are listening but you're not hearing me*. That missing part has evaded me for so many years.

In 2021, I started joining adoption groups, as I was writing my biography and decided to write this story of my adoption as a book in its own right, as it's been such a huge sticking point in my life. I began to see posts about feelings that were the same as mine, more and more in particular from older adoptees and some younger adoptees with exactly the same missing links in their growth, processing of life events, etc. The eureka moment was epic. I felt for the first time in my life I belonged somewhere that people could actually answer me with some degree of empathy, sympathy and knowledge. I could say things that sounded weird to others that have not been adopted without feeling like a complete waste of space for even opening my mouth.

Over many years I have felt like I was the worst Christian on the planet, not being able to manage my feelings and retreating into self-preservation mode on many occasions. There was a season where I was told repeatedly I was negative and had a critical spirit. It may have been true, but I now understand that I was still operating in fear and a lack of understanding about my own issues. Rejected, unwanted, not good enough. No matter how hard I tried to get myself together and join the crowd, I was never fully part of the crowd; always looking in from a distance, hearing stories of parties I was not invited to, weddings where I wasn't on the guest list, people having dinner parties I was never invited to. I thought, *why would anyone want a negative, critical person like me at their house anyway?*

I was failing as a Christian too. The one good thing I was certain about was that no matter how many people rejected me for whatever reason, I knew wholeheartedly that God loved me in every fibre of my being and, when I only had that one thread left, that's what I clung to.

I remember being at a meeting with some of the leadership of the church, as we were in leadership – yes, even me with all my issues, was in leadership. We were being encouraged to be better in our areas of ministry and looking at one day being licensed ministers. At one point someone said to me and Brian, "Yes, Brian could certainly fill a church, but you Fiona would empty it!" It may have been said in jest but, to me, this sentence held me back for years. I constantly recoiled from doing anything that would put me in that position. Being a pastor's wife was never going to be something that was attainable to me, if I was truly such a bad person that I could empty a church. I was fully aware I had issues and could be fairly blunt. I was never going to put myself in a position where I could ultimately put people off going to church or becoming a Christian.

I noticed some of you raising your eyebrows there about the fact that, as a Christian, I still had a missing link or two or three. I want to make it abundantly clear here that I am most definitely a born-again, blood-washed, Spirit-filled Christian. I know that Jesus Christ died and rose again and that I might have eternal life. I also know I wasn't fully healed in the area of my adoption issues. I have at the point of writing this sentence been walking the Christian path for more than twenty-five years. In my book *This is Me: No Darkness too Deep*, I detail my point of salvation and my journey through the early years of being a Christian and how I walked through so many obstacles. It also details my years caught up in drug addiction and being crippled emotionally by events brought about through my lifestyle over my early teens and twenties. Most of those can be traced back to the moment of being given away, and then again, and trying to settle in a family where, unfortunately, I was the middle child.

So, walking through Christianity, I had so many issues that needed to be worked through. In time these issues were worked through by a very loving and patient God, who ministered to me bit by bit. The Healing Rooms in London were one of the most fruitful places where I received healing from God. Betty and Tom Burke and the team have an incredible ministry that has led to so many people being healed by God. My husband Brian and I did the training and began to volunteer in the Healing Rooms. We were not married at that point but, before we got married, we had a session with the team, who prayed and we were moved in an incredible way and prepared for our coming together. We have been together for nearly twenty years.

There is certainly hope for those that are adopted and struggling with the feelings they are going through. As an older adoptee, at fifty-five years of age at the time of writing this book, I feel that there is certainly more that should be on offer for us as we try to iron out the wrinkles in our lives, never mind the physical wrinkles we still need to deal with at our age. So I hear you ask: what are the remedies to this trauma, this issue, these feelings we are struggling to manage?

I can only share with you what has been working for me in these last twenty-five years. The first thing I can say that has definitely been a great help to me is my faith. I pray and take great comfort in the word of God. There are a couple of scriptures in particular that have ministered to me over the years. In fact, the first time I read the word "adopted" in the Bible, I was amazed. *Oh my gosh*, I thought, *adoption is in the Bible*. Moses was adopted, for example. There are other references:

Psalm 68:5-6: A father to the fatherless, a defender of the widow, is God in his holy dwelling. God sets the lonely in families

Ephesians 1:5: In love he predestined us to be adopted as his sons through Jesus Christ, in accordance with his pleasure and will.

Oh wow, I thought, *I've now been adopted by Jesus*. When I first read the scripture in Ephesians, it was a nice feeling to know I had been adopted by Jesus. There was no chance he was going to be abandoning me any time soon; more likely, it would be me trying to shake him off, as I had all my life, avoiding that full heart and soul commitment and connection with someone or somewhere.

I have lived in Manchester for over eighteen years, going through fourteen house moves in that time for one reason or another, and really like the city. We currently stay in the house we have lived in for almost five years, so what does that tell you about my level of moving around in thirteen years! Moving doesn't faze me. I'm not sentimental about things and soon forget what may have been left behind. Is this linked to me being adopted or is it just the way I am? I can't answer that – it could be either or both.

Defining those moments where the problem was that I was adopted, or that I was just made that way or reacted that way because it was in my temperament, was always difficult. As I got older and learned a bit more about myself, I would learn that I had certain ways of responding or reacting to triggers. My heart was always turned towards those that were less fortunate, the downtrodden, the beaten, those that struggled to get on in life. I've always had a soft heart for those that are struggling with their identity and struggling with life issues. I know how it feels; I have been there and back.

Getting Married – AGAIN!

Getting married or hooked up with someone has never been an issue for me. When I was married, I was always completely faithful. Unfortunately, I didn't receive the same faithfulness back.

So, multiple failed relationships and two failed marriages later, I suddenly found myself in love with a young man called Brian, thirteen years younger, half a foot smaller and with the most glorious red hair. We got married after a very short courtship which took our church completely by surprise. Many were the doom and gloom brigade that said it would never last: it was all too fast, she was old enough to be his mother. This was such a challenging time for me, with so much bad feeling being directed at me. For what? Falling in love? For knowing without a shadow of a doubt that God had called us together?

It was awful. Off we went up to bonnie Scotland to tie the knot, with our families all doing well to not show that they weren't sure either about this unlikely duo. We got married on a Wednesday and, the day before, we prayed with each other that if any of us woke up in the morning with any doubt that this was from God, we were not going to turn up at the wedding. Unfortunately, on the day, my car was late and the boughs fell off on the way, so I was nearly twenty minutes late. Poor Brian must have been thinking the worst. I woke up with no doubt whatsoever this was the man God had called to put up with me for the rest of our natural lives.

Our marriage was no bed of roses. We had our issues, like everyone else. I was bossy, or a bully as Brian would say, and he was so indecisive that it would drive me to distraction. The first few years of our marriage, I would flounce out the door vowing not to come back and it was over. I did my utmost to bring Brian to the end of himself so that he would go and have an affair, as the others had. Our sex life was incredible – we were both quite adventurous and had plenty of experience (sorry, family, if that's too much information).

My insecurities with close connections were kicking in big time. I loved this man fiercely and knew he loved me. The jealousies and fears were all kicking in and it was getting tense. I must have told Brian I was leaving about 100 times when it all came to a head one night after yet another pointless row about nothing (yes, even Christians fight in their marriages). The threat of divorce was being thrown at Brian yet again. One of the amazing things God does when he brings people together is to match them perfectly. Brian sat down on the couch and began to cry.

All the wind blew out of my sails really fast as I looked at him with a big tear rolling down his face.

"I don't want you to go," he said. "I need us to sit down and talk some stuff through."

That night he shared some of his deepest fears and insecurities. We prayed, and I vowed never to say I was leaving and flounce out the door again.

Infertility

The word infertility has followed me around since I was nineteen. I never fell pregnant with my first husband or with my second husband naturally. All the tests with both partners revealed they had supersonic sperm. The problem lay with me, and it was called unexplained infertility.

I had been pregnant at seventeen but had been badly beaten and lost the baby at twenty weeks. I had a womb, a cervix and ovaries that ovulated perfectly well every twenty-eight days or so. Could I fall pregnant? No, not even a whiff of a pregnancy.

At twenty-nine in marriage number two, we went through the IVF programme. We lost twins. I vowed never to go through that again as it was the most horrible process. During my first marriage I decided to look for my natural family, in case there was a genetic issue somewhere along the line. It turned out that everyone else in that family was extremely fertile – it was just me!

In both marriages, we spoke about adoption and I was completely against it, as I knew how difficult I had found it. Even though I understood things had progressed a bit since the 60s and 70s and there would most likely be good support for any adoptee, I couldn't face deliberately putting a child through what I had gone through as an adoptee.

Marriage number three was the same, though I did think, with God on our side, it would not be long before we heard the patter of tiny feet. Alas, again, we went through the barrage of tests that anyone who has faced infertility knows all too well. Once again everything was working fine, with all moving parts in good working order. Once again we were sent off to keep trying as it was unexplained infertility.

We went to all sorts of lengths to have a child: reading all sorts of books, changing our diets, and we must have been prayed for in thousands of places. I got to the point where if the pastor said I want to pray for all those that want to have children and can't, I would cringe inside and not want to go down again for prayer. God most obviously was not going to give us our heart's desire.

As the years went by, I prayed, I believed. Still nothing. We even went through a stage where Brian would pray immediately after each attempt. That had to stop – it kind of took the afterglow moment away. We were asked to pray for a couple we had been friends with that had been married a year or so and were trying for a child. Six weeks later she called to say she was pregnant; they now have four children. I joined up with two other women in the church who desperately wanted children. We met regularly, shared our disappointments and even bought each other a gift for our future babies, in faith. Both women went on to have children and I was left on my own peeping into my drawer every so often to hold my newborn's vest and baby grow. Misery reigned for a couple of years watching people having their babies, being genuinely happy for them, but having a huge sadness for myself and for Brian. We had been trying for a good few years with no results, and loads of months where a day late would result in yet another pregnancy test being bought and thrown away in despair. I should have bought shares in the company.

Back to the doctors we went, blind faith exhausted. So the barrage of tests began again. It was time to find out the results of our tests. There is nothing nice about sitting in that waiting room looking around at the other anxious couples sitting, waiting to be called in.

"Mr and Mrs Myles." It was our turn, and we held hands and walked down the corridor with the nurse, willing there to be some hope. It was not to be. We received the hammer blow that day that my eggs were effectively dead. I was only forty-three. The menopause had started fairly early.

I watched the pain draw all the colour from Brian's face. My own emotions were clattering all over the place. I felt pain for myself. I was agonising for my husband because there was nothing we could do. Our options were to use someone else's eggs or adopt. The consultant was trying to be nice, but also was trying to shuffle us out the door. There was a waiting room full of couples waiting to be seen. I don't think either of us wanted to leave the consultant's office, as that would to us be absolute when the door closed behind us.

We walked out the door, down the stairs and out into the brightness of daylight. The silence between us was loud. Cars were whizzing by, people were passing, on their phones, couples were laughing and kissing as they went by us. It was all so loud.

I've no recollection of getting to the bus stop or getting on the bus. We went up the stairs and sat down at the front. I looked at Brian's white face and asked him if he was OK. He burst into tears right there on the bus. He cried quietly for a while and I resumed my silence. By the time we were almost home, he was slowly regaining colour. I kept feeling like I had to say sorry all the time. It was completely my fault that my husband now knew we were never going to have children. Not the best feeling I've had in my life.

We got into the house where we were living with six of the young women from the church. It was a lively house and refreshing to be with the youth, but that day we needed a clear run to our room. Thankfully, they were all out or in their rooms. As soon as we got into our room, we collapsed to the floor on our knees and prayed like we never really had before. We had a house full of women that we loved dearly. We knew some of them were at crisis points in their own journeys, so we needed to pray this out. We did share with the house in the morning at our morning devotional time, which brought a bit of healing.

Where did we go from there? I needed to be reassured that I wasn't going to lose yet another husband to someone else because he wanted children. I was also painfully aware Brian needed to get his head and his heart around this news.

Life went on. We spoke about adoption, about fostering, briefly about saving up the thousands of pounds we would need to buy an egg! Sounds lovely, doesn't it, to buy an egg, not knowing really where that egg comes from, just that it's a match, intellectually, physically, etc. Things moved on. We moved on. Our church and ministry was very fast-moving and, when you're working closely with people, it can be very easy to focus on their needs and not your own.

Fast forward a couple of years to 2014. I am the director of the Victory Outreach Manchester Women's Home – something that has been the desire of my heart for over ten years. We had moved into the position within the ministry the year before and were loving it. We were living with the women, leading them into a journey with Jesus Christ and teaching them to pray and build their own relationship with God and others. The women had all come from drug addiction and were willing to trust God to set them straight in their path of life. We had a conference called Victory Outreach World Conference. These are huge events and I had been praying daily that God would give me a word to continue on in the home.

At the conference, God spoke to me very clearly at the altar that He would give me a child at fifty! It was a mind-blowing moment where I was sure he had said it but strangely doubted it, given my circumstances. I had been fully through menopause and I was now very settled in the women's home. When we got back from the conference, I had to tell the church what God had said. Around this time, someone from the church came to me and said they wanted to have a baby for us. My heart was so touched and I thought that maybe this was the baby God was promising. We prayed about it and knew it was not the way that God wanted us to go.

Again time marched on, still with no sign of any child, and I was only getting older. In August of 2015, my mother sadly died. It has to be the most painful moment of my life, standing by the hospital bed with the rest of the immediate family watching her breathe out her very last breath. That instance of complete finality of life right in front of our eyes. We were quietly and quickly ushered out while the nurses did what they had to do. Going back into the room to see my mother before we left her at the hospital was awful. She was dead and looked dead; not like in the films where they look so sweet and not dead. My heart was broken; my family's hearts were broken. I had talked about the promise I had been given to Mum, and she was completely convinced I was mad to even want to start a family at fifty, but she was also looking forward to me not being the only childless person in the family.

The finality of having no parents except for my stepdad was hard to get through, with no parents and no children. Mother's Day 2016 was the hardest day I had to get through, grieving the loss of my mother and, as always, grieving the fact I had no children. As part of a very busy, thriving church, these events were marked with gifts and children running to their parents with little flowers or chocolates after service. Mothers were being asked to come down the front to be prayed for, new mums were giving testimony. There was also the dreaded 'let's give the infertile people a flower too'. Sorry if that sounds awful but, if I'm honest, I liked that part the least. Walking out of service with my flower or whatever was a reminder I was not a mum. I feared being missed out on that list, because then it was a double indignity of not being a parent and also not being acknowledged as not being a parent. How on earth does a church or group setting get that balance correct? My personal journey of rejection meant that nothing would make it feel any better. It was one day out of the year that I prepared for and dreaded, but knew I needed to brave the day. I wasn't alone; my situation was unusual, but I was not on my own. My biggest struggle was articulating what it felt like to be childless for all those thirty-plus years. Of course, I was happy for all the young and not-so-young mums that were steadily building the church, one child at a time. Did I feel awkward at baby showers? Of course I did. Did I avoid them? Yes. There were times when I was feeling my own sense of loss more than others, so I couldn't attend some of them. It was never that I didn't want to; it was just too hard.

Things were about to change: God was about to blow my mind. My sister was getting baptised. I hadn't really seen much of her since my natural mum died in 2005. I decided to surprise her on the day and travelled to the baptism. It was such a beautiful day. I stayed with her overnight and she began to tell me about her granddaughter, who was about to be put into the care system. My spirit was leaping. It was May 2016. I turned fifty in March. This was our child; this was our promise. It looked impossible to us that we would be considered for this child. We both had criminal records, had both been drug addicts, were running a Victory Outreach Women's Home full of addicts and this little child had been born a drug addict. Her withdrawals had been severe; she had a brain bleed at a day old. She had been with her foster carers since coming out of hospital after five weeks. She was allergic to everything. Well, maybe not everything, but she was on anti-seizure medication and the doctors had said she may not walk and, developmentally, she may not go beyond five years of age.

We went into the process firmly believing this was our promise. We had just got our first appointment for assessment when Brian was diagnosed with testicular cancer. What a blow. Would this stop the process? We continued on through Brian's battle and chemo. Our little princess, our promise from God, was placed in our house on the 13th of January, 2017, exactly six weeks before I turned fifty-one. Mother's Day 2017 was going to be epic.

God had moved. He had spoken, and given me the promise I had given to the church. I had no idea how he was going to bring this about but he was already preparing our child. She was from my own bloodline; a small part of me is in her. She had red hair, a small part of Brian. When God does something, he does it properly. Over many years as a Christian, I walked sometimes in a place of bewilderment as to how people heard from God every day, had life-changing moments, heard life-changing messages every week, went to altars and testified how God had shown them this and then that. I very often went to the front and stood very sincerely waiting for my life-changer touch or revelation, then skulked back to my seat feeling a bit jealous of everyone else that was getting weekly 'things' from God. I maintained my prayer life and reading in the hope I, too, would be having such great relations with God.

Was I not submitted enough? Was my walk not sincere enough? Maybe there was some blockage because I was adopted, so I didn't receive the same as other people. I used to try to seek out other adoptees, and found a similar trait in people who had been in care or had fractured family upbringing. That fear of the ultimate rejection from God was almost too much to even think about. I found it almost impossible to completely abandon myself to God in case I found myself once again abandoned. My prayer life would be centred on continuing to go on with him, always asking him to bring me to that place of complete abandonment, watching people move in their place of abandonment and wondering what that feels like, watching others struggling in their walk and not being able to help them as I knew I was struggling in the same way, being unable to express my feelings again through that fear of being discarded as not good enough.

Having my daughter, being a parent, being so loved by God that he brought about this series of events to honour the promise he gave me, you would think I would now be in the realm of super-Christian, testifying all over the place, laying hands on people in prayer, being used in a mighty way by God. But things were going in the opposite direction. My prayer life was dwindling fast, to just the necessary amount of prayer to keep the flames of hell from singeing my bottom. Needless to say, being a parent was not what I had thought it was going to be. Loads of parents had given me advice, told me it was going to be tough, but I thought, *this is my promise; it's going to be different for me*.

Guess what? It was no different for me; it was hard. My daughter was on the go non-stop from 5 a.m. She would start to make noises. She never stopped moving while she was awake, always going from toy to toy and back again. We had to be super-careful with everything she ate as she had multiple allergies. We had many a dash to A&E with sudden, bright rashes. Everything was super-scary for me. I loved being a mum, but looking after our little bundle of joy was exhausting. Brian and I would put Georgie to bed at 7 p.m. and smile fondly at her as we gently closed the bedroom door. We would make ourselves a nice cup of tea and relax on the couch. Most nights we woke up with neck strain at 10 or 11 p.m. still sitting on the couch with a cold cup of tea waiting to be sipped.

Every part of our lives totally changed, and we had no outlet with Georgie. She was so sensitive to foods that an allergy could happen at any point. Bath products were an issue, wipes were an issue, some materials were an issue. She never stopped: from waking to sleeping, she constantly needed to move, touch and explore. It had been explained to us that she may not be able to walk and there would be developmental issues. Brian was determined she would walk and, while I was at work and he was still off work recovering from chemotherapy, he worked tirelessly to show her and help her get to her feet. The day that I came home from work and she took two steps towards me was one of the most momentous moments of joy I have felt in my life.

We decided to have Georgie dedicated to God at church. We also had her prayed for at a Wednesday night prayer meeting regarding all the allergies she had. From that day she was able to tolerate dairy and eggs and continued on in being able to manage lots of things that were new to her. We discovered she was allergic to penicillin after giving her a dose of it for an infection. Yet another dash to A&E with Georgie's face puffed up like a balloon and her gasping for breath.

Life continued with our little ball of fire. She has the most explosive temper that flares up fast but also simmers down fairly quickly too. Getting her place at nursery was brilliant, and it was super getting her off to nursery for the day. She did two days for a while and then qualified for four days. It became apparent very quickly that she was not doing well at nursery, and was losing her temper, lashing out and being very aggressive towards staff. We were told it was just bad behaviour and to try to teach her what she seemed to be missing. We had no clue what was missing. The same thing kept being said: she was a super-friendly, happy little girl but with these seemingly random explosive, aggressive moments. She was always happier outside and that's where we often found her when picking her up. On many an occasion, we had to pick her up early for one reason or another.

School was looming. It was said that she may struggle to settle at school. September 2019 to February 2020 were by far the most awful six months of my parenting journey. My child was distressed, unhappy, violent at home and at school. In early October, I got a call to go pick her up as she had been excluded from school for her and the staff's safety! She was still only four years old. What was troubling her so much? The school was incredible with her and the special educational needs (SEN) staff got on board quickly, sorting out an Education Health and Care plan, which should already have been in place. They worked very hard to help her manage her time at school, but she did have another term of exclusion. I had to navigate meetings with multi-professionals over and over again. Getting help was difficult but there was a determination in me to get the best for my little girl.

In the midst of it, I knew it was crucial to initiate a WhatsApp prayer with a chosen group of men and women to cover my child in prayer while we navigated this new place. I struggled to connect with the other mums as I knew that most of their kids had been at the end of Georgie's tempers. It wasn't really until the last couple of months of the school year that I started to say hello to other mums, as Georgie was doing a lot better and I didn't feel so awkward. We came to the decision she would fare better in special education. There was a small unit with only six places available that we all felt would be perfect for Georgie; the prayer team were on it and we got a place for her.

This is where we are at with our little gift from God. She started at her little SEN unit in September 2021. I believe she will thrive. Yes she will struggle at first, because she has general difficulty in transition to new things and struggles to express herself. She is and can be fairly incontinent at night in particular, when she is upset and unable to explain what's upsetting her. When she was very small, she would EXPLODE in her nappy when in a new situation or unhappy. Thankfully she can control that now, but does have the odd explosion at night if she's very upset.

As I write this, she is almost six years old. Her mode of expression is to peel the paint lovingly painted onto her walls by her dad off the walls and the door. But it's not her that's doing it: it's Charlie and Charlotte, her dolls. Have I ever wanted to give my gift from God back to Him? Hmmm, maybe I had brief moments of *I don't think I can cope with all of this*. But never have I wanted to give up on my little poppet.

Our marriage is eighteen years old, and fourteen of those were childless, yearning for a child. Those fourteen years were not easy: we managed thirteen house moves, and only one house did we have more than one Christmas in. We struggled through abject poverty; literally having nothing to eat. We had huge rows and health issues over the years. I had a mental breakdown in 2010 which led to some long-lasting issues. We battled cancer and ran a women's recovery home for four years. Nothing prepared us for the hit our marriage was going to take when Georgie arrived. My third and final book about my life is called *This is Me – In My Marriage*. There, I open up the vaults of stories and testimonies of what we have endured in our years of marriage. Sometimes people kindly say that you have such a lovely relationship with your husband, and inside you're thinking, *you come and live with him for a while*. None of us is easy to live with. We gaily skip up the aisle with the love of our lives, not realising they are human too. I'm blessed to have Brian as my husband and the father to our daughter. It's been a roller coaster of a ride in our marriage.

So let's look at me in my marriages. Yes, I said "marriages". I have been married three times. My first marriage was in 1985 to Simon. This marriage was a complete disaster. There was infidelity on his part. There was violence and madness on both our parts. This marriage was drink and drug-fuelled, which didn't make for any fairy tale ending. We did have some very memorable times living in Southern Ireland like hippies, a bunch of young men and women, smoking weed and going down to the river singing Woodie Guthrie and Bob Dylan songs by the open fire, while fighting off midges and wasps. There was no bath or shower in the decrepit building we were living in so we went down to the river and washed in that. Sounds fairly cool, but it was freezing and many a time I would come out with a dirty great leech on my leg! This marriage ended fairly quickly and we were divorced by 1989.

A few failed relationships later, I married again, this time to Tam. He was nice and fairly mild-mannered and enjoyed a smoke of weed and a wee drink. We had many good times and many not-so-good times. I was by this time not a very nice person, through alcohol. In this marriage, I came to Christ. Tam did his best to come to church to see what I could see. He simply didn't get it. He never experienced Christ as I did.

One of the most significant moments in our breaking up was when we were in a caravan in Northern Ireland that my friend let us stay in to try to help us. Tam had been drinking quite heavily and things were not going well. We went for a walk to try to calm our situation down. I couldn't understand how he would not prefer this non-drinking, much calmer, more peaceful wife instead of the raging lunatic I had been before. Tam could not understand what had happened to me and, in a moment of heated discussion, he threw me into a hedge, leaning over me shouting that he wanted his wife back. I knew at that moment, as the hedge thorns pierced the skin on my back, that our marriage was not going to make it.

We went home and just meandered along, but on decidedly different paths. Tam was still not interested in going to church or anything. He resented the change in me. I couldn't read my Bible in front of him. There were lots of issues around me going out to church and to meetings and things. Eventually, I came home from an early morning prayer meeting to find that he had left me. I had stayed over at my friend Brenda's that night to go to the meeting. As soon as I walked in, I knew he had gone. I had no idea where he had gone, but he had taken our bed, washing machine and other bits and pieces that were essential.

I found out the next day that he had moved in with a woman he had been having an affair with who was pregnant with his child. I was devastated. I loved my husband and had really hoped that one day he would come to find the faith I had found. I had no income that would sustain the flat and no way of getting the things I would need to keep it. I didn't want to live in the flat on my own anyway. The church helped me to move in with a lady who had a spare room for a while until I got a house of my own.

I was now officially single, which was not something I had ever really been for any length of time. How was I going to navigate this as a Christian? Honestly, I didn't think I was going to manage it; I don't like living on my own. I was happy that I had a house, but was now struggling with being lonely and fearful on my own at night. I sought advice about how to overcome these feelings. Pray about it, seek God about it, ask him what you should do going forward. I decided to take women into my house as lodgers and then went on to bring street women in to detox them from heroin and send them on to the Teen Challenge programme in Wales. I had lots of great characters that came to stay with me, and I thrived on having people in my house and praying with women.

Over the years, I went out with the odd guy here and there. One or two came into my life and I wondered if they were The One? It even got very close to marriage with one suitor; seven weeks away from the wedding, I believed God was telling me he was not the man for me. I was blown away but could not shake off the knowledge this man was not who God had intended for me. I was very flattered he had gone out with me and declared that he loved me and all the things we want to hear. He had a great job, great income, his own lovely house in a lovely place. I obediently called a halt to going through with the wedding. To say that my decision didn't go down well is a bit of an understatement. I will draw a line under that right there.

I was single again, but this time I still had my house. I still had women coming through. The church had a bus we went out in once a week to reach out to the addicts around the town. We gave testimony and soup. We decided to have an evangelistic crusade to highlight the bus and what we were doing. A team came up from London Victory Outreach headed by Paul Lloyd, a gifted young man, who had a great desire to see people reached by the gospel of Jesus Christ. The team were incredible. They were all ex-addicts bar one. They went out to the schools, and the team did street work with the bus in many locations and saw many men and women head to their recovery facilities in London. One of those young men that happily skipped off to drug rehab was Brian Myles who, unbeknown to me, was destined to become husband number three.

Brian had come into the church through the crusade as a six-stone heroin addict. He had come to the end of himself after a failed attempt at suicide.

The crusade was over. I felt sadly deflated. I had loved the buzz of the Victory Outreach group being with us. I knew that was my group of people, but I stayed at my own church for over a year after that and then knew God wanted me to be at Victory Outreach. I had visited and spent a month in the home before I upped sticks and closed my house, moving down to London.

Let's get to the bit where Brian and I start to realise that we like each other. We are now living in a shared Christian house with lovely big rooms and a lovely garden. We are both working in the Good News Bookshop in Leyton, a nice, short walk from the house, with no nasty commuting to work through London. We got on fairly well as friends, went out together fairly platonically, just hanging out and eating together after work. I found him funny and sweet but not husband material. He was far too young for me; I do prefer an older fella in general.

Life went on settling down into my church. I found it very hard to settle into the new way of doing things, and there were lots of new people to navigate and get on with, or not, as the case may be. Hence spending time with Brian was always a nice experience. I wasn't short of admirers and was asked out on more than one occasion, which was always a nice distraction. No Mr Right yet, though. I did really like someone in the church and I kinda knew that they liked me too. It was a bit of cat and mouse, as none of us wanted to admit the attraction. In my mind, I was trying to work out if it was physical or spiritual – was he The One or not? I've never minded going out to dinner with someone on a 'date' if I knew they may not be The One, as it's just a meal to me, and not to be repeated unless there are signs it is more than that.

Time marches on. Days and weeks went by and I began to feel feelings for Brian, which surprised me a bit because he was not my type. I had never once in my life prayed for a small redhead from a different generation! I had, however, always prayed for a man that loves the Lord, is a giver and a lover of the Word. I knew two of these were true of Brian and I went to the finance guy at the church to find out if he was a regular tither and giver. I was not disappointed.

During these weeks and months, we both had interesting experiences with possible partners. Brian was invited to a church picnic by a pastor's daughter but, unfortunately, I had a funeral to go to. When the girl in question's dad came into the shop, Brian very politely apologised for not being able to go to the picnic with his daughter. The dad was confused and said there had been no church picnic. Lucky escape for Brian, who never saw the girl again.

I was invited by a lovely man to run away with him and live on his boat. That one still makes us both laugh to this day. This guy basically worked around the corner and got the bus every day outside the shop. He would wave and smile at me. He came in a couple of times to buy random small items and chat. Then the big expose. Flattered as I was to be asked to go and live on his boat with him, I was a little dubious, as he didn't even have a car.

Eventually, I got to the point where I knew I loved Brian and was in love with him. It was a strange experience. We had been so close, working and living together without any romantic feelings being involved. I knew in my heart I had to tell him, to give him the opportunity to either accept what I was saying or move away from the closeness of our completely platonic relationship up to this point.

Biting the bullet over our dinner that evening, I told him I was in love with him.

To say it didn't go down well is a bit of an understatement. Brian simply got up and left the table to go to his room. I didn't see him all that evening. In fact, I hid in my room feeling very insecure and vulnerable, trying to work out what on earth he must have been thinking and would he ever speak to me again? I was in turmoil. I knew I had to say something because I knew my motives for hanging out with him had changed dramatically, so felt it only right to mark that boundary.

The next morning was agonising, waiting to see if he would wait for me to walk to work as per usual. He was there and we walked to work as usual but, unusually, he did not mention what I had said and I didn't broach the subject. I had to pray and leave it with God.

Life went on and I started to enjoy spending time with another guy in the church I knew liked me. He asked me out eventually and was waiting to take me out after work one day with a lovely bunch of flowers. Brian saw him and asked what was going on. I told him we were going out for something to eat. Brian let me know the guy was still married. Even though they were not together, it still changed things for me. Bearing in mind I've lost two previous husbands to infidelity, it's not something I would ever want to do or be a part of, even in a small way.

With a heavy heart because I was actually very hungry, I went out to tell him I would not be going out with him because I now knew he was married. He gallantly put up a mediocre protest, which I appreciated. I knew he was not The One.

One Sunday a few weeks later, I got up early, prayed and read my Bible. I was feeling very positive. Our housemate Barry had, as always, asked me to iron his work shirts for the week, which I did and hung them up on the living room door as usual. Church service was good. As I made my way home I heard the meep-meep of Barry's moped. He was a character; I loved him as a brother. He had expressed that he wanted more, but I didn't feel that way about him. Brian was just being dropped off at the house as me and Barry arrived home full of giggles. He went in the house first, went straight up to the beautifully ironed work shirts and threw them on the floor! He stood on them and declared I would never iron another man's shirts again! It was such a shock to me and Barry; we gawped at him, wondering what was going on.

Barry and Brian started shouting the odds at each other and I slipped off to my room. What did all that mean? What had happened to Brian? Did he actually like me? Was this too-good-to-be-true stuff? My heart was hammering listening to those two downstairs hurling insults at each other. Everything went quiet and I heard them both slamming into their rooms. I ventured out for a takeaway dinner and ate in my room. Falling asleep, I continued to pray about the situation that had now become very tense all around.

I woke up to my room door knocking. Who was at my door in the middle of the night? It was really only 10 p.m. and I had been sleeping for ages. I opened the door to find Brian standing there with a very serious face on him. He declared to me that he was just letting me know we would be getting married! It took all my self-control not to burst out laughing at his seriousness. I just said quickly, "No way until you ask me properly," and slammed the door on him.

Long story short – Brian proposed beautifully in the Healing Rooms of the Good News Shop in Leyton with Betty as a witness. It was such a strange courtship, if it could even be called that, and now we were going to get married. It was October 2003. We decided our wedding would be in January 2004.

One of my greatest regrets is that we had sex before we made it to the altar. We lived in the same house and spent all our time together. I had very little accountability with anyone in the church as I hadn't really got that close to anyone. It also really didn't help that it all unsurprisingly came as a bit of a shock to the whole church, as we were not even a couple but were now suddenly getting married.

The age gap was fairly noticeable: I was thirty-seven and he was twenty-three. I took a good bit of flak from some of the younger women I can only assume had their eyes on him and were upset. There was also one, in particular, that gave us both a very hard time over it all, even going to the point of writing Brian a letter to say how upset they were and that he was making a mistake. We weathered the storms by getting too close and falling into bed together. Brian moved out until after the wedding. I remember my pastor asking us, pre-wedding, if we had been sexually active. I felt shame and regret having to honestly say we had.

The wedding was amazing; the day was great. We had a hotel booked for us by a friend in Edinburgh as my natural mum couldn't be at the wedding as she was having radiation treatment for cancer. We visited her the next morning with our wedding clothes on. The rest of the week was spent doing evangelism and we gave our testimonies at the church on Sunday night before we went back to London to start back at the shop on Tuesday. It was the shortest week ever.

Married life had started. Things were about to get rocky very quickly. We were happy at our work. Betty had made Brian manager a few months earlier with a very generous wage and she had put me more on the admin and wages side of things, again with a very generous wage. We got an invitation to dinner with our pastor and his wife. They had a proposal for us: would we consider going to Manchester to help with the restart of the Victory Outreach there? It did come as a bit of a shock, as we were only married a couple of months. We went away and thought about it and decided to make the move, after much prayer and deep thought.

In the first year of our marriage, we went from exceptionally high earners to having no money at all. We were struggling to pay our rent, eating meagre amounts of food and trying to find our way in a new church with new people in a new city. We didn't make a big thing of our struggles: we had been sent to help, not cause more stress.

Eventually, things panned out and we reached an even keel. In the midst of it all, we were put to work in the church helping in almost every area. I worked very hard for four solid years building up the administration and doing the church accounts ready for submission at the end of each year. It was difficult and very stressful managing the admin and the accounts. I did recruit a few people to help as and when they could. It was full-time for me but without a wage. I was given an allowance of £50 a week which covered my travel and lunch. I also had a job working nights in a home for adults with learning difficulties. Brian was working for Wesley Owen. We were managing OK.

Our struggles to have a child were a very trying time, going through a battery of tests over and over with no real cause being established. For me, I had lost a child at twenty weeks and had a failed IVF, losing twins. I had an early-term miscarriage in 2006.

Life went on and we went on to direct the men's home after a sudden departure. Rolling into 2008, we were asked to take on a huge seven-bed house in Moss Side as a young women's discipleship house. We had a great time doing that for a whole year, with loads of laughs and great times of fellowship. As Christians, we were doing it all to serve God and thoroughly enjoying it as well. We had made some lovely friends and were very happy.

During our time at the Keswick convention that year, Brian had been praying about his career; he wanted to go up the ladder in Wesley Owen. He knew at this point he was not going anywhere in ministry terms. He had a burning desire at one point to be a pastor in our ministry but some circumstances had wiped that desire out of him. He did love his work and felt better equipped at that time to pursue promotion for growth. He prayed and we prayed and God opened doors that only he can open. It was incredible. We moved down to London for Brian to start in a senior position in one of the London stores. I was given a job in the administration department, which meant, once again, we were in the high-earner category. I was happy, Brian was happy. It was all about to come crumbling down around us.

At work one day Brian came to tell me that Betty had called him and wanted him to go back to work for her in the Good News Shop in Leyton. She offered him a great package to go back. I was dubious as it wasn't what God had given him. We didn't agree on him moving but he went anyway. He loved Betty; she had nurtured him and loved him through so much in the time he had worked for her before. To say the manager was angry was an understatement. I thought he was going to punch Brian in the face when he told him. It was so tense and uncomfortable that, after a couple of weeks, I felt I had to leave as well.

I knew in my heart this was a huge mistake. We also needed to move; we lived nowhere near Leyton. Our pastor offered us a room at his place, where we lived for a few months before we made the move back home to Scotland. A catalogue of disasters had resulted in us upsetting our pastors in Manchester, upsetting friends in Wesley Owen, leaving Victory Outreach thinking that when God had told us to go home that meant to go where we both considered home: Scotland. I felt betrayed by everyone and everything, even by God. Brian was desperately unhappy, I was desperately unhappy. We had no money and were walking round to Morrisons to see what things were in the 'whoopsies' and living off soup and bread. We didn't qualify for benefits because Brian had left a perfectly good, highly paid job to go to Falkirk, where there was high unemployment. Our dear friend Marcia came up often and paid our rent and bought us food. We will be eternally grateful to God for giving us such a good friend.

The breaking point came very quickly. I could not cope with the pain I was feeling. I felt let down by God and deep anger towards Brian for accepting the move to Betty's. I was never in doubt about the move to Wesley Owen in London. I believe that move was 100 per cent from God. The end result of us being at crisis point was not being obedient to what God had wanted us to do.

Through every other thing we had to deal with, we had the ever nagging infertility issues going on. It was month after month of misery and not seeing that positive result, ever. I should have bought shares in pregnancy test companies; I used thousands over the years.

Eventually, we decided Brian would go back to Manchester. Our marriage wasn't surviving and he was deeply unhappy in Scotland. I was very happy to be home. I knew very quickly that I needed to join him. He was my husband and I loved him; I was just deeply angry with him.

I didn't particularly want to go back to Manchester; we had been away just over a year. It felt very strange and painful being back for me, as I knew we had gone from being in the centre of everything to being on the outskirts of the church looking in. Our friend John McQuarrie gave us his basement to stay in until we got our own place. We struggled to find our feet together, but we knew we were meant to be together. It took a while, but we got a little house and began to build again.

The stress of everything caused me to have a nervous breakdown, which was one of the most frightening things I've had to go through. I lost the plot on a bus, through fear and confusion, and had to be taken to hospital. I was prescribed heavy medication for a while. Brian would go to work with me sitting on the couch in my dressing gown and come home from work and I would still be sitting exactly where he left me. Some days I could not even wake up before he left, so he would come home to find me still in the bed. After a couple of months of this, Brian asked me to stop taking the tablets as I was just not able to function. I did stop taking them and, after a week or two, began to see clearly again. I believe my brain just needed a rest.

Life rolled on and things were good between us. Financially, we had taken a big hit while I had been unwell. I didn't have a job and had not been able to get one and Brian was working part-time. Our rent had been paid, but from credit cards, along with council tax, water, electricity, the list goes on. We maxed out on everything and the interest was piling up. We lost the house and ended up staying with friends again. Our debt had racked up to over £21,000, and a huge proportion of that was interest. CAP (Christians Against Poverty) were incredible; they got us all sorted out with affordable monthly payments and we both managed to find work. We soon moved into our own place again. Things were going very well. We were happy, had a lodger, cats, and all was fairly normal and settled. Once again we were working together in Gorton Market.

My heart's desire was to run a women's recovery home for Victory Outreach one day and, after all we had been through, I was beginning to doubt this would ever come to pass. Christmas 2012 brought about a conversation with the pastor and his wife asking if I would step in as home director in early 2013. My heart's desire was about to come to pass. Running the home full of women with addiction problems and lots of other issues was a huge task. We lived in and were on hand 24/7 to sort out any issues. We managed the budgets, managed the women with the help of lots of lovely volunteers that would spend time with the women to give me a break. Brian worked full-time but still supported and brought great fun in the evenings and weekends.

In February 2014, Brian found an ominous lump in his groin. It turned out to be a hernia he had to have surgery for. Before this hernia was discovered and removed, we had enjoyed a very good, healthy sex life. After the surgery, Brian suffered serious nerve damage which resulted in it not being possible to manage sex. Just as things were beginning to get better and there was the hope of a return to normal service, I discovered a lump in his testicle. He was quick to brush it off as nothing, but that thing grew really fast and he knew he had to get it seen to.

Sitting in that room waiting for the consultant to tell us if it was benign or malignant was like an eternity. We had prayed and pleaded for it to just be a lump. We had prayed for the strength to deal with it if it was malignant. The consultant very gently told us it was cancer and he would need surgery straight away and then chemo.

Brian burst into tears at that point. I was at a loss as to what to say. A specialist nurse was ushered in to explain all that was about to happen. Thankfully, it was stage one, which meant the best chance of it being dealt with completely. Surgery and chemo left Brian in a poor state; it was a very difficult time for us.

We were in the process of coming out of the women's home after almost four straight years serving God, building women of God. It was again a very tough time financially and emotionally. Our marriage again was under enormous strain. Our sex life never returned after the surgery and chemo and, as I write, we have still not enjoyed each other again. That's not to say we have not loved each other – we just haven't been able to know each other.

In 2018 I had my own light brush with cancer where, during a scan for something else, it was found that I had a small growth in my womb that was pre-cancerous. I went through a huge operation, being opened up from side to side to remove everything. I then became completely unable to manage anything intimate. I don't even know right now if I can manage anything intimate. Things have got to the point where we have become very comfortable like this. Our marriage has taken some knocks over the years, we have gone through some tough times but have always known that, above all else, God brought us together in the strangest of circumstances and it's only God that has kept us together in the good and not-so-good times.

Our journey through our marriage has always been with the dark cloud of infertility over us. That yearning, that crying-at-night misery of not having a child. The agony of watching every friend you know having children, no problem at all, praying for other couples struggling to conceive or walking with them through the pain of miscarriage, but then always sharing the ultimate joy with them of having a child or two or even three. That joy continued to elude us.

In summer 2014, at a huge Victory Outreach Conference in America, I heard God tell me I would have a child at fifty. It came as a bit of a shock. I was not having sex as we were unable to. I had actually stopped ovulating three or four years earlier as well, so the impossibility of it seemed too much to imagine. We were running the women's home at the time, and I began to imagine that maybe one of the women in the home would have a baby and leave the baby with us. Maybe God was going to miraculously open my womb, as he had done with Sarah. All sorts of crazy scenarios were going through my mind.

In May of 2016, my sister became a Christian and was getting baptised. We had not had much contact for a while, but I was happy to hear about it from my other sister. I travelled to see her being baptised. It was a big surprise to them all when I walked in. We did so much catching up that night.

She began to tell me about her son's little girl, who was with foster carers and quite poorly after being born addicted and suffering a brain bleed which kept her in hospital for the first five weeks of her life. She was needing a forever home as she was not going back to her parents. My spirit leapt in my heart. I knew this was our child. I went home and explained it all to Brian and he was of the same mind.

The odds were stacked against us: we were living in a house full of addicts, both had criminal records and had both been addicts. Things began to progress and we passed through the initial interviews and mandatory checks. Social workers were giving us the right sounds that we were going to be put forward to have Georgie. The journey was not without its bumps in the road as this is right when Brian was found to have cancer. It was during his chemo that we met her for the first time. I can remember him being so exhausted that day that he slid off the couch onto the floor. The day that we met Georgie, I didn't take my phone with me, I left it in the B&B. I wanted nothing to interrupt my connection with Georgie. We connected immediately and it was the most wonderful day. Things were going to move very quickly and we could possibly have her with us by Christmas.

When I got back to the B&B, my phone had loads of missed calls from my family. My stepdad had been found dead in his flat that morning. It was such a sad end to what was the most beautiful day connecting with our soon-to-be daughter.

There were a few glitches to come in the lead-up to everything being finalised but, on the 17th of January 2017, our little girl was placed in our care. Remembering that God had told me I would have a child at fifty, Georgie was placed with us just six weeks before my 51st birthday.

I kept remembering the Sunday after the conference where I was prompted by the Holy Spirit to tell the whole church that God had told me I would have a child at fifty. I really didn't want to but knew, as I said the word out loud, that I had to. I had no doubt that this would come to pass. I had no idea how it would come to pass. Never in my wildest dreams did I think God would in advance make a way for us to have a little girl, from the family I was adopted out of, as our child.

She looks very like me and has Brian's red hair. Our journey into parenthood had begun. Let me tell you right now that when people tell you it's not easy to parent well, they are telling the truth. When people tell you your child will grow up very, very quickly, you need to believe them and take every moment to build your connection, relationship. Please don't waste a moment. Our little poppet is six years old and it has flown by.

We have navigated her being allergic to almost everything in the beginning. We were told she may or may not walk; she runs rings around us. Brian was off work for a few months when we first got her as he recovered from his surgery and chemo, and worked tirelessly with her to get her on her feet. We had our pastor pray for her multiple allergies and she was healed of most of them. She has a nut allergy and an allergy to penicillin. Georgie suffers from complex needs, ADHD, developmental issues and skin problems. She's still incontinent at night, and during the day if she is very anxious.

Georgie is not adopted, but we are starting the process very soon. She has a Special Guardianship Order at the moment. She is most definitely our little girl, whom we adore. She is as quick as a flash with her cheeky replies. She eats like a horse and never stops talking. She loves a big adventure and is a complete outdoors girl. She wants a dog, but we need a house first. If you pray, please pray for us to get a house with a garden so wee Georgie can get a dog.

Whether you as the reader believe in God or not, I do, and I believe my husband and I are still together because of our relationship with him. I most definitely heard God tell me I would have a child at fifty, and I did. As for God healing me from all the issues that being adopted throws up, I can say that, yes, he has helped me come to terms with the emotional turmoil. I still do naturally feel instantly rejected and not wanted by people, but I know straight away that I am loved unconditionally by God, which gives me peace. That is something no one can change. I get my strength and peace of mind from God, but I still speak to people in groups about my feelings around being

adopted. I have a group on Facebook called This is Me –
I'm Adopted. Come in and join us.

Thank you to all my readers for supporting me as I've
written my story. I am truly grateful to every reader. Please
don't hesitate to contact me about anything in this book.
Also, if you want to read part one of my story, you can
find it on Amazon: *This is Me: No Darkness Too Deep*.

THIS IS ME
Fiona Myles

This is me Fiona Myles born in the mid-sixties. I am' married to the amazing Brian a gorgeous redhead. We have one daughter called Georgie who is five and one son Connor who is 21.

Manchester has been our home for the past 18 years a fabulous metropolis full of energy and history.

I started writing stories from a fairly young age. My Mum bought me a typewriter when I was around eight or nine years old. I battered away at that little typewriter, day in and day out, for a while. Life moved on and so sadly did the typewriter.

Fast forward 45 years and the birth of the laptop which becomes my new typewriter. My passion for writing was reignited during the awful time of the national lockdown in 2020.

This is Me – I'm Adopted is a testimonial book of my roller coaster journey through life.

I do hope that this book has been inspiring and helpful. Please do get in touch with me or any of the agencies below if you have any questions or concerns.

There are lots of agencies and groups where you can share your experiences of adoption and other issues:

Adoption UK: www.adoptionuk.org

Adoption Matters: www.adoptionmatters.org

AdoptionChatter on Instagram

Facebook group: This is Me – I'm Adopted. Helping with Adoptee Mentorship courses to walk you through making changes in your life.

If you have marriage issues, contact Relate, other charities or speak to your minister/pastor for referrals. Don't just give up on your marriage/relationships.

Relate: www.relate.org.uk

Care for the family: www.careforthefamily.org.uk

Connect with me

Instagram

Fionamylesauthor

Facebook

Fiona Myles Author

Check out my AdoptionDesigns shop at Redbubble

Visit my website: www.fionamylesauthor.com

Email me: fionamylesauthor@gmail.com

www.marciampublishing.com

Printed in Great Britain
by Amazon

86536770R00050